T0112388

My First Bible

Mercè Segarra
Illustrated by Armelle Modéré

Good Books®

Creation

God created the world step by step.
The first step was to create light
in the daytime and darkness at night.
Secondly, He created the sky,
the seas, the mountains, the trees
and the flowers.

Thirdly, He created
the sun, the moon
and the stars.
Fourthly, He created
the animals.
And in the fifth
and final step,
He created humans
to love the earth.

Adam and Eve

The first man and the first woman that God created were called Adam and Eve and they lived in a marvelous place: The Garden of Eden. God told them they could eat the fruit from any tree, except the one in the very middle of the garden.

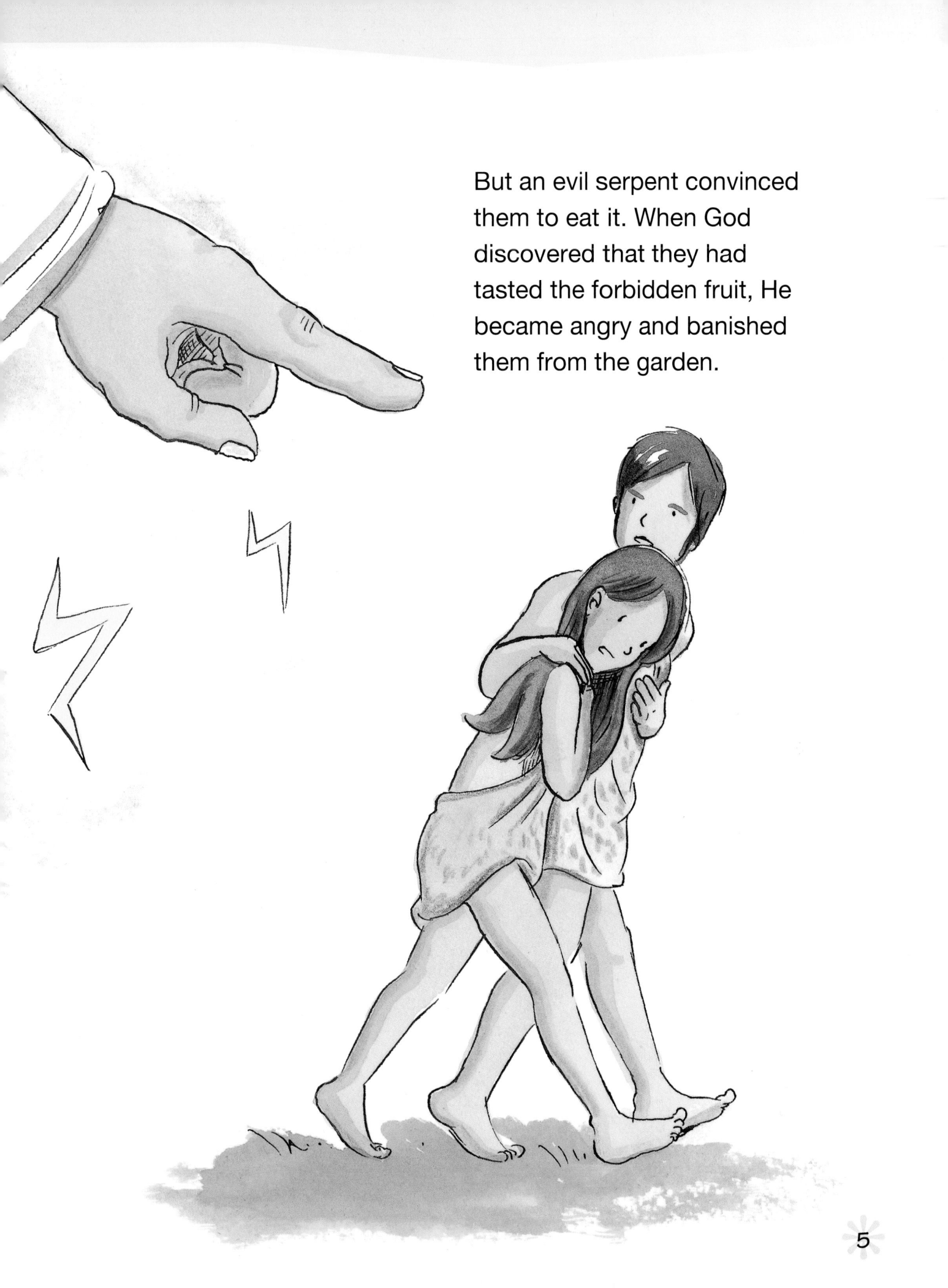

But an evil serpent convinced them to eat it. When God discovered that they had tasted the forbidden fruit, He became angry and banished them from the garden.

Building the Ark

The earth became ever more populated. Many people were not good and they forgot about God, except for Noah.

God asked him to build a large boat, an ark, because He was going to flood the earth, but Noah and his family could save themselves.

Flooding the Earth

God asked Noah to board a pair of each kind of animal onto the ark, as well as himself and his family.

Then it rained for forty days and forty nights and everything was flooded. But Noah, his family and the animals were safe, because they were in the ark. When it finally stopped raining, they left the ark. And as a promise that He would never harm the earth again, God made a rainbow.

Abraham and Sarah

Abraham and Sarah were a married childless couple of advanced age. One day, God told Abraham to go and live in another place, which He would indicate to him.

Abraham obeyed and together with his wife took their sheep and goats and they began the journey to an unknown destination.

Isaac

One night, Abraham heard God tell him:
"This is the earth, which I give to you
and your children."
"But I have no children," replied Abraham sadly.
"And I can't have any now. I'm too old."
"Look at the sky, Abraham. Can you see the stars?"
Abraham nodded.
"And can you count them?" God asked him.
"No. Nobody can," replied Abraham.

Then God said to him:
"Listen to me carefully, Abraham. You will have a son and you'll have grandchildren."
God kept his promise. One year later, Sarah had a son called Isaac.

Esau and Jacob

Isaac and Rebecca had twin sons, called Esau and Jacob, who were very different from one another. When Jacob grew up, he decided to live in his uncle's house very far away.

One night, while traveling, he slept resting his head upon a stone and he had a dream: He saw a long ladder that reached up to the heavens and angels going up and down. God was at the top and He said to him: "Jacob, I will never abandon you. And also, I will give you lots of children and land." From that day onwards, Jacob was never afraid again.

Joseph

Jacob had twelve sons. One was called Joseph, and Jacob loved him so much that he gave him a very beautiful tunic.

His brothers were jealous of him.
So, one day, while the flocks were grazing, they robbed him of his tunic and sold him to some merchants who took him far away, to Egypt.

Joseph in Egypt

While Joseph was in Egypt, God protected him. Also, He gave him the ability to interpret the meanings of dreams.

One day, the King of Egypt (the Pharaoh) summoned him, because he wanted to know the meaning of two dreams he had had. They meant that Egypt would have seven years in a row of good harvests, followed by seven years of poverty and famine. Joseph advised him to store up the food during the seven years of abundance to feed the people when the years of poverty arrived.

When the period of famine arrived, Jacob sent all his children, apart from Benjamin, the youngest, to buy food in Egypt.

Joseph's Brothers

Joseph saw them and without revealing to them who he was, he asked them to go and get their younger brother. When they were all together, he told them who he was and forgave them for what they had done to him in the past. In the end, they all went back to Egypt together.

Israelites in Egypt

After several years, there was another Pharaoh in Egypt who hadn't met Joseph.

This Pharaoh was afraid, because many Israelites had come to Egypt in search of food and many of them were powerful. To stop them from rebelling against him, he decided to enslave them and also ordered for all the Israelite male children to be thrown into the river.

Moses

An Israelite mother had a son and she didn't want to throw him into the river. So she made a straw basket, placed her son inside and put it in the river.

The basket floated away until it got stuck in some reeds. The Pharaoh's daughter found it and decided to keep the child and bring him up as if he were her son. She named him Moses, which means "drawn from the water."

Bush in Flames

When Moses grew up, he discovered that he was an Israelite and not an Egyptian. When he saw how his people lived, he decided to escape from the palace and go to the desert.

When he arrived, he saw a burning bush and went closer.
Suddenly, he heard God say to him from the bush:
"Go back to Egypt and ask the Pharaoh to free the Israelites."
Moses obeyed, but the Pharaoh didn't want to free them.

Leaving Egypt

Since the Pharaoh didn't want to free the Israelites, God decided to punish the Egyptians by sending them plagues. When the Pharaoh saw this, he was frightened and let the Israelites leave. Then Moses guided his people to the Promised Land, or the Land of Canaan. This departure from Egypt is known as the Exodus.

When the Israelites left Egypt, the Pharaoh's army followed them. When they reached the Red Sea, the Israelites didn't know how they were going to cross it.

Splitting the Sea

But God sent a very strong wind to help them and the next day, they found a path between two walls of water. So, they were able to cross the sea and reach the desert.

God Gave Bread

Although the Egyptians had fled, the Israelites wandered through the desert exhausted from thirst and hunger.

Moses asked for God's help and He promised them that bread would fall from the sky like rain. And so it was: It rained bread called manna, which tasted like wafers made with honey.

The Israelites reached Mount Sinai.
One day it was covered with mist
and there was a great storm.

The Ten Commandments

God called Moses and He gave him two stone tablets with the laws the people of Israel should follow. These laws were called the Ten Commandments.

The Ark

God ordered His people to build an ark, a kind of chest, to hold the tablets with the Commandments.

While they traveled through the desert, the Israelite soldiers watched over it and when they stopped, they placed it in a tent decorated with tapestries. For them, it was like a temple, where they prayed and worshipped God.

The Horns of Jericho

After many years, Moses died and God chose Joshua as Israel's new guide. His mission was to lead his people to Canaan.
The first city they reached was Jericho. They were unable to enter, because it was surrounded by very high walls. Then God told Joshua to walk around the city blowing horns. They did so for six days and on the seventh, the walls fell down and they were able to enter the city.

Samuel

The Israelites conquered those lands, but they were not always good people. God gave Israel some guides (the judges and prophets), who helped the Israelites to follow the path of good.

The last of these guides was Samuel, who ruled for many years. When he grew old, he chose his children to govern, but the people were tired and asked him to choose a king for the people.

Saul

Samuel chose Saul as the first king of Israel. Saul was very strong and defeated many enemies.

But the people stole things,
kept them and didn't share
them with anybody. God
was not pleased with this
and He asked Samuel
to choose another king.

Samuel chose the young shepherd David as the new king. David was very brave and he fought Goliath, who was a giant from the enemy army, feared by everybody.

David and Goliath

David beat the giant and was a good king. He made Jerusalem the capital of his kingdom and God helped him.

King Solomon

When David died, his son Solomon
became the new king of Israel.
He asked God for wisdom,
because he wanted to rule well.

As he was not asking for material goods,
God was pleased and gave him many riches.
To thank Him, Solomon built a temple
in Jerusalem dedicated to God.

Daniel and the Lions

Daniel was a great prophet. He lived in the court of the king of Babylon, where he was a counselor. In Babylon, the people worshipped false gods and there was a law that punished anybody who failed to worship them.

As Daniel was loyal to God, he was punished. They threw him into a pit of lions. But he was not afraid, because he trusted that God would protect him from the lions. And they did not harm him. Thus the Babylonians realized that Daniel's God was the true God.

Jonah and the Whale

God asked Jonah the prophet to go to Nineveh and ask the people to be good. Jonah didn't want to go and he boarded a ship to escape.

While he was on the ship, there was a great storm and Jonah realized that it was his fault for not listening to God's orders. So, he asked for the sailors on the ship to throw him into the sea. When he fell into the water, he was swallowed by a great whale. He asked God for forgiveness and God forgave him.

The Annunciation

One day, an angel appeared before Mary, who lived in Nazareth, and told her that she would have a son and that he would be called Jesus.

Mary excitedly went to see her cousin Elizabeth, who was also pregnant. Elizabeth was the mother of the last prophet, John the Baptist, who prepared the hearts of the people for the arrival of Jesus.

The Birth

Mary married Joseph, who was a carpenter. They both went to Bethlehem.

After a long journey, they were very tired and looked for a place to stay, but they couldn't find anywhere, because there were a lot of people. Luckily, a man let them sleep in his stable. Jesus was born that night.

Good News

The night when Jesus was born, some shepherds were sleeping in the countryside near Bethlehem. Suddenly, the sky lit up and an angel appeared before them and told them that a baby had been born in Bethlehem and that he was the savior. The shepherds hurried to go and see him.

The Kings from the East

Far away from Bethlehem,
in the East, there lived
three very wise men.

One night, a very bright star appeared before them and they thought that it was a sign from God, so they loaded their camels and followed the star, which led them to the stable where Jesus was born. They worshipped him and gave him gold, incense and myrrh.

Jesus and his family lived in Nazareth.
When Jesus was twelve years old,
his parents took him to Jerusalem to
celebrate Passover.

Jesus in the temple

When the festivities were over, everybody went home. Mary and Joseph thought that Jesus was among the people who were returning. Then they realized that he was not with them, so they went back to Jerusalem to look for him. They found him in the temple, speaking with the teachers, who were teaching people things about God. Jesus asked them about God and they were impressed by how he spoke.

The Baptism

Jesus's cousin, John the Baptist, lived in a desert. One day, while he was in the River Jordan, encouraging people to be good and baptizing them, Jesus appeared and he asked John to baptize him.

While John baptized him,
God spoke, referring to Jesus:
"This is my son."
That's how everybody discovered
that Jesus was the son of God.

The Disciples of Jesus

Jesus knew that the time had come to travel the land and teach that God loved everybody and to ask people to love each other.

He needed men to help him to spread these messages. So, he chose twelve helpers, most of whom were fishermen, who he called disciples.

The Wedding at Cana

Jesus and his disciples were invited to a wedding. While Mary was helping with the wedding, the wine ran out.

Then Mary asked her son to do something, because she felt sorry for the bridegroom and his family. Jesus performed his first miracle: He converted six jugs of water into very good wine. Henceforth, his disciples believed and trusted him more.

Jesus Heals the Sick

Jesus traveled throughout the world for three years.

Every time he reached a city, he was greeted with great enthusiasm, because he had the power to heal the sick, just by touching them.

Jesus was also known for telling beautiful stories about the love of God: the parables.

The Parables

Each of these parables had a message
for the people to be good and understand
that God loved and forgave everybody.

Parable of the Two Sons

A man had two sons and he asked the elder to go and work in the vineyard owned by the family.

He replied that he didn't want to go, but later, after thinking about it, he regretted his answer and decided to go and work. The father did the same with the younger son, who quickly replied that he would go to work straight away, but in the end, he didn't go. Which of the two sons followed his father's will?

Parable of the Two Houses

Jesus said: "He who listens to my words and puts them into practice is like the sensible man who builds his house by digging the foundations in the rock.

The rain fell, the wind blew, torrents crashed against the house, but it was not knocked down, because it had good foundations. However, he who listens to my words and fails to put them into practice is like the foolish man who builds his house on the sand. The rain fell, the wind blew, the torrents crashed against the house and it collapsed, because it did not have good foundations."

Parable of the Grain of Mustard

Jesus also said to his friends:
"What I want from you is for
you to be a grain of mustard.

When it is sown, the mustard is one of the smallest seeds on the earth, but when the plant is born and grown, it becomes the largest of all the plants in the garden. Its branches grow very long and the birds of heaven take refuge in its shade."

A shepherd had 100 sheep and he lost one. He left the other 99 and went to look for the one that had gotten lost until he found it.

Parable of the Lost Sheep

Then he returned home very pleased
and gathered together all his friends
to tell them the good news.

Jesus and the Children

One day, some parents took their children to Jesus, so that he could bless them. But the disciples told them that Jesus was very busy.

Jesus saw that the parents and children were very sad and he got angry with the disciples. Then he blessed each of the children.

To Jerusalem

One spring, Jesus and his disciples went to Jerusalem to celebrate Passover.

Jesus rode on a donkey and the people greeted him with branches of olive and palms. He was very moved to see everybody adoring him and he entered the city like a king.

The Betrayal of Judas

The high priests thought that
Jesus had power over the people
and they wanted to kill him.

Judas, one of Jesus's disciples, did not love him and he didn't understand him either. So, he told the priests where they could find him, in exchange for thirty pieces of silver.

The Last Supper

Jesus knew that he was going to die soon and he wanted to celebrate the last Passover supper with his disciples. Although he was sad, he tried to hide it and encouraged them to love one another as he had loved them. During the meal, they drank and ate bread. Jesus told them that whenever they gathered together for Passover, they should remember him.

After the supper, Jesus went to pray in an orchard at the Mount of Olives.

The Olive Grove

Some of the disciples followed him.
Suddenly, Judas appeared with the high
priests' soldiers and they arrested Jesus
and took him to Pontius Pilate, the governor.

The Crucifixion of Jesus

Pontius Pilate asked Jesus whether he was the son of God and he said yes.

Pilate wanted to free Jesus, because he though that he had done nothing wrong, but the high priests wanted to kill him and Pilate listened to them. Finally, Jesus died after being crucified on a hill outside the city.

The Resurrection

Jesus' friends buried him in a cave and sealed the entrance with a great rock.

Three days later, three women went and saw that the stone had been moved. Then an angel appeared before them and told them that Jesus had been resurrected and they went running to the disciples.

The Ascension

After coming back to life, Jesus appeared to his friends on several occasions.

One day, he explained to them that he was about to go up to heaven with God, but he promised them that he would send them the Spirit of God, who would help them to be strong and to tell his story and spread his message of salvation to the people. Several days later, a holy fire came down to rest on the shoulders of his disciples. It was the power that Jesus had transmitted to them to help them spread what he had taught them throughout the world.

Copyright © 2009, 2020 by Mercè Segarra

Originally published in English by Gemser Publications, S.L. in 2009.

First Good Books edition, 2020.

All rights reserved. No part of this book may be reproduced in any manner without the express written consent of the publisher, except in the case of brief excerpts in critical reviews or articles. All inquiries should be addressed to Good Books, 307 West 36th Street, 11th Floor, New York, NY 10018.

Good Books books may be purchased in bulk at special discounts for sales promotion, corporate gifts, fund-raising, or educational purposes. Special editions can also be created to specifications. For details, contact the Special Sales Department, Good Books, 307 West 36th Street, 11th Floor, New York, NY 10018 or info@skyhorsepublishing.com.

Good Books is an imprint of Skyhorse Publishing, Inc.®, a Delaware corporation.

Visit our website at www.goodbooks.com.

1 0 9 8 7 6 5 4 3 2 1

Library of Congress Control Number: 2019950485

Text by Mercè Segarra
Illustrations by Armelle Modéré
Design and layout by Gemser Publications, S.L.

Print ISBN: 978-1-68099-491-9
Ebook ISBN: 978-1-68099-492-6

Printed in China